QUESTIONING HISTORY

THE EMANCIPATION PROCLAMATION

Asking Tough Questions

by Nel Yomtov

Consultant
Tim Solie
Adjunct Professor of History
Minnesota State University, Mankato
Mankato, Minnesota

CAPSTONE PRESS
a capstone imprint

Capstone Captivate is published by Capstone Press, an imprint of Capstone.
1710 Roe Crest Drive
North Mankato, Minnesota 56003
www.capstonepub.com

Library of Congress Cataloging-in-Publication Data is available on the Library of Congress website.
ISBN: 978-1-4966-8469-1 (library binding)
ISBN: 978-1-4966-8815-6 (paperback)
ISBN: 978-1-4966-8489-9 (eBook PDF)

Summary: What was the Emancipation Proclamation? How did it affect the South's ability to fight in the American Civil War? How did it change the lives of enslaved black people? These questions and others are examined to inspire critical thinking for young readers.

Editorial Credits
Editor: Aaron Sautter; Designer: Sara Radka; Media Researcher: Eric Gohl; Production Specialist: Kathy McColley

Image Credits
Alamy: Pictures Now, 16, PJF Military Collection, 32; Getty Images: Ed Vebell, 27, Picturenow, 12, Robert Abbott Sengstacke, 42, Stringer/Fotosearch, 31, Universal History Archive, 25, 39; Granger: 11, 17, 36; Library of Congress: cover (back), 24, 29, 33, 45; North Wind Picture Archives: 5, 8, 9, 19, 20, 30, 35, 38, 41; Pixabay: MIH83, background (throughout); Shutterstock: Blue Planet Studio, cover (front), chrupka, 15, Everett Historical, 7 (right); Wikimedia: Public Domain, 7 (left), 21, 23

All internet sites appearing in back matter were available and accurate when this book was sent to press.

Printed in the United States
PA117

Table of Contents

Words in **bold** are in the glossary.

Did the Emancipation Proclamation Keep Its Promise?

WHY WERE BLACK PEOPLE ENSLAVED IN AMERICA?

Slavery existed in the United States before America even became a country. The first European settlers brought enslaved black people to North America in the late 1500s. For more than 200 years, hundreds of thousands of people were taken from their homelands in Africa. They were crammed into slave ships with little food, water, or fresh air. Thousands died on the journey to the American colonies.

Those who survived were treated as property. Some enslaved black people were traded for goods like sugar and molasses. But most were sold for money. They provided most of the labor on **plantations**, especially in the South. Enslaved black people did the backbreaking work on these farms. They planted and harvested crops and took care of animals. They did the cooking and cleaning, maintained buildings, and did many other hard jobs for white enslavers.

The life of an enslaved black person was a living nightmare. White enslavers thought of black people as less than human. They treated their slaves however they wished. Enslaved black people were often punished severely. Beatings, whippings, and torture were common for those who broke the enslavers' rules. Even those who followed the rules suffered greatly. They faced endless hard work, poor nutrition, unclean conditions, and disease.

Enslaved black people were often packed onto ships by the hundreds. Many died from lack of food and water or from disease.

WHY DID PRESIDENT LINCOLN WRITE THE EMANCIPATION PROCLAMATION?

The end of slavery in America began with the Emancipation Proclamation. The Proclamation was written by President Abraham Lincoln. He wrote it in the middle of the American Civil War (1861–1865). It took effect on January 1, 1863.

The document freed enslaved black people in the states that were part of the **Confederacy**. Once freed, Lincoln believed slaves would refuse to work for white enslavers. He hoped this would upset the South's economy and the war effort. He also hoped that black people would join the **Union** army.

FACT

Slave codes were laws in the South. They stated what enslaved black people could and could not do. Enslaved people could not own property. They were not allowed to read or write. They couldn't meet in large groups, testify in court, or own guns. And they couldn't strike a white person, even in self-defense.

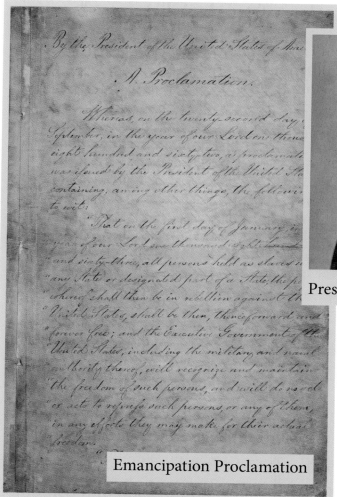

Emancipation Proclamation

President Abraham Lincoln

The Emancipation Proclamation is one of the most important documents in history. But it is also one of the most misunderstood. What events inspired Lincoln to issue it? What did Lincoln hope it would accomplish? What did it fail to achieve? In the following pages, we'll take a deeper look at these questions and others involving the Emancipation Proclamation.

CHAPTER 1

How Did Slavery Lead to the Civil War?

WHY WAS AMERICA A DIVIDED NATION?

By the late 1850s, the United States was a divided nation. Slavery was important in the South. Nearly 90 percent of enslaved black people lived in southern states. They provided the labor needed to keep the South's economy strong. Laws in the South gave white Southerners a legal right to enslave black people and treat them however they wished.

Enslaved black people did the backbreaking work of harvesting crops like cotton on plantations.

Slavery was not widespread in the North. Most Northerners opposed slavery and thought it was wrong to treat people as property. Over time, northern states had passed many laws to end slavery. Many people felt it was time to end slavery in the South too. **Abolitionists** and supporters of slavery had strong disagreements.

The arguments eventually led to the Missouri Compromise of 1820. Missouri joined the Union as a slave state. Maine joined as a free state. The law kept the balance of slave and free states. It also banned slavery north of Arkansas. The law kept the peace for a time. But in 1850 Congress had to work out a new deal. The Compromise of 1850 allowed California to join as a free state. Meanwhile, the Utah and New Mexico territories were allowed to choose to be slave or free states.

The Compromise of 1850

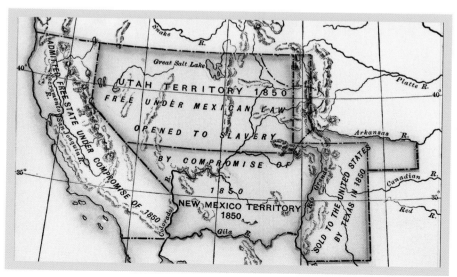

WHAT WAS "BLEEDING KANSAS"?

The laws passed in 1820 and 1850 didn't settle the issue of slavery. In 1854 Congress passed the Kansas–Nebraska Act. It canceled the Missouri Compromise of 1820. It allowed white people in Kansas and Nebraska to choose if slavery would be legal. Violent conflicts between pro- and anti-slavery forces soon broke out in Kansas. This period soon became known as "Bleeding Kansas." Hundreds of people fought over the issue of slavery. Many were killed.

HOW DID SOUTHERN STATES REACT TO LINCOLN'S ELECTION?

Abraham Lincoln was elected President in November 1860. Lincoln felt that slavery was a great evil. But he promised not to take action against slavery where it already existed. Southern states didn't believe him. Shortly after the election, South Carolina **seceded** from the Union. By June 1861, 11 Southern states had left the Union. They instead formed their own country. They called it the Confederate States of America, or the Confederacy.

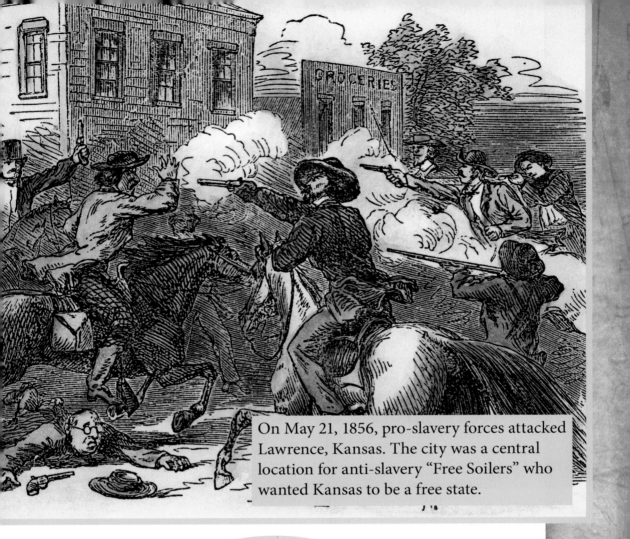

On May 21, 1856, pro-slavery forces attacked Lawrence, Kansas. The city was a central location for anti-slavery "Free Soilers" who wanted Kansas to be a free state.

FACT

In 1850 Congress passed the Fugitive Slave Act. It required that all enslaved people be returned to their owners, even if they were found in a free state. The law outraged many Northerners.

HOW DID THE CIVIL WAR BEGIN?

On April 12, 1861, Confederate forces attacked the Union's Fort Sumter. The Civil War was on. On July 21, the first major battle took place at the First Battle of Bull Run in Virginia. Southern forces scored a major victory over disorganized Union troops. The Confederacy believed it was fighting for the right of the states to choose to be a slave or free state. Firm in their belief, the South scored a string of victories early in the war.

The first battle of the Civil War took place at Fort Sumter. It was a Union sea fort in Charleston, South Carolina.

Enslaved Men at the First Battle of Bull Run

White soldiers weren't the only ones to fight at the First Battle of Bull Run. John Parker and three other enslaved black men also fired upon Union soldiers. They had been ordered by white enslavers to fight. During the war, many enslaved black people were forced to build walls and do other hard work in Confederate camps.

Important Dates in the Civil War

April 12, 1861: Confederates open fire on Fort Sumter; the fort surrenders the next day

July 21, 1861: The First Battle of Bull Run; Confederate victory

August 10, 1861: Battle of Wilson's Creek; Confederate victory

October 21, 1861: Battle of Ball's Bluff; Confederate victory

March 9, 1862: Two ironclad ships, the C.S.S. *Virginia* (Confederate, previously U.S.S. *Merrimack*) and the U.S.S. *Monitor* (Union), battle to a draw at Hampton Roads, Virginia

June 25–July 1, 1862: Seven Days Battles; Confederate victory

August 28–30, 1862: Second Battle of Bull Run; Confederate victory

September 17, 1862: Battle of Antietam in Maryland; ends in a draw

September 22, 1862: Lincoln announces Emancipation Proclamation

January 1, 1863: the Emancipation Proclamation takes effect

July 1–3, 1863: Battle of Gettysburg; Union victory

April 9, 1865: Confederate General Robert E. Lee surrenders to Union general Ulysses S. Grant at Appomattox Court House, Virginia

WHAT CHALLENGES DID PRESIDENT LINCOLN FACE IN HIS FIRST YEAR?

Few U.S. presidents have faced as tough a challenge as Abraham Lincoln. The country was split in two as soon as he took office. Lincoln did not want to fight a war. But he was determined to keep the Union together. Early in the war, Lincoln struggled to find an effective commander for the Union army. He grew frustrated by the Union's increasing losses on the battlefield.

Union free state

Union slave state (Border States)

Slave state seceding before Fort Sumter, April 1861

Slave state seceding after Fort Sumter, April 1861

Territory

Meanwhile, Lincoln was also criticized by Northern abolitionists. They urged him to use his authority to declare all enslaved people free. Still others in the North urged Lincoln not to take hasty action against slavery. They supported the war only as a way to **restore** the Union. They had no desire to free enslaved people.

United States vs. Confederate States, 1861

New Hampshire
Vermont
Maine
Minnesota
Massachusetts
Dakota
Territory
Wisconsin
New
York
Michigan
Rhode Island
Connecticut
Nebraska Territory
Iowa
Pennsylvania
New Jersey
Ohio
Delaware
Illinois
Indiana
Maryland
Colorado
Territory
West
Virginia
Virginia
Kansas
Missouri
Kentucky
North Carolina
Tennessee
Indian Territory
Arkansas
South
Carolina
Mississippi
Alabama
Georgia
Louisiana
Texas
Florida

Lincoln also had to act carefully with the Border States. Delaware, Kentucky, Maryland, and Missouri were slave states. But they didn't join the Confederacy. Lincoln couldn't risk them joining the South by taking any action against slavery. If they did, the South would be too strong.

WHAT WERE LINCOLN'S VIEWS ON SLAVERY?

Lincoln opposed slavery. But his main goal at the start of the war was to preserve the Union, not to free enslaved people. He expressed his views in a letter written to the *New York Tribune.* "If I could save the Union without freeing any slave I would do it, and if I could save it by freeing all the slaves I would do it . . . ."

In 1858 Abraham Lincoln and Democratic Senator Stephen A. Douglas held several debates about slavery in Illinois. Lincoln felt the federal government had a duty to end slavery. But Douglas felt that new states should be free to choose to be slave or free states.

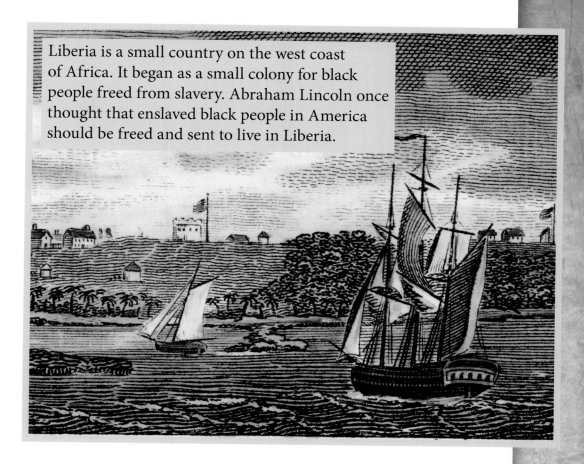

Liberia is a small country on the west coast of Africa. It began as a small colony for black people freed from slavery. Abraham Lincoln once thought that enslaved black people in America should be freed and sent to live in Liberia.

Lincoln had long struggled with his personal opinions about slavery. He believed slavery was unjust and evil. He felt that enslaved black people were ripped from their homeland. He thought they were victims who had been brought to America against their will. But he was uncertain about the best way to end what he called "a great wrong." During the 1850s Lincoln thought that enslaved people should be freed gradually. He thought they should be sent back to Africa or encouraged to start their own settlements overseas.

CHAPTER 2

How Did President Lincoln Decide to Issue the Proclamation?

DID LINCOLN TRY OTHER WAYS TO END SLAVERY?

In the fall of 1861, President Lincoln created a plan to help end slavery. The U.S. government would repay states that agreed to free enslaved black people. Lincoln first made the offer to the four Border States. He hoped that if they accepted the offer it would weaken the Southern states and they would stop fighting. The same offer could then be made to the Confederate states. However, none of the Border States accepted Lincoln's offer. The plan failed.

But Lincoln wasn't ready to give up. On April 16, 1862, he signed the Compensated Emancipation Act. The law freed about 3,000 enslaved people living in Washington, D.C. White enslavers were paid $300 for each enslaved person. The act also set up a fund to help newly freed black people move to a foreign country.

On April 19, 1866, thousands of people gathered in Washington, D.C., to celebrate the anniversary of the Compensated Emancipation Act.

FACT

Washington, D.C., is the capital of the United States. During the Civil War it was known as the District of Columbia.

Union forces suffered heavy losses during the Seven Days Battles in 1862. General George B. McClellan ordered his army to retreat across the Chickahominy River in Virginia.

WHAT FINALLY PUSHED LINCOLN TO TAKE ACTION?

Lincoln's first goal was to keep the Union together. But he still wanted to see the "ultimate extinction" of slavery, as he said in 1858. By the middle of 1862, he became convinced that ending slavery was a moral duty. Yet he still hesitated to act.

On July 1, 1862, Union forces were defeated in the Seven Days Battles near Richmond, Virginia. Discouraged by another Union loss, Lincoln met with Major General George B. McClellan. The general gave Lincoln a letter he had written. McClellan was opposed to fighting a war to free enslaved people. The letter suggested that Union forces might refuse to fight if Lincoln tried to end slavery.

McClellan's letter shocked Lincoln. The president realized that freeing enslaved people could no longer wait. It could not be done gradually. He had to take steps now while he was still the president.

Union General George B. McClellan

FACT
Union general George B. McClennan wanted formerly enslaved black people who had escaped to work in the army. He wanted them to help move his troops, wagons, and supplies. However, he thought that white enslavers should be paid for their loss.

?

HOW DID LINCOLN JUSTIFY HIS DECISION?

As president, Lincoln had certain war powers granted by the U.S. Constitution. Lincoln believed that the South would be weakened if the enslaved people were freed. But no one was sure that his war powers included freeing them. Lincoln worried that U.S. courts could rule that his plan was **unconstitutional**. He proceeded with it anyway.

On July 22, 1862, Lincoln presented the first draft of an Emancipation Proclamation to his advisors. Lincoln wrote that it was "a fit and necessary military measure." The document ordered "that all persons held as slaves . . . shall then, thenceforward, and forever, be free."

President Lincoln shared the first draft of the Emancipation Proclamation with his cabinet in July 1862. From left to right: Edwin M. Stanton, Salmon P. Chase, Abraham Lincoln, Gideon Wells, Caleb Blood Smith, William H. Seward, Montgomery Blair, Edward Bates.

Secretary of State William Seward had one major concern, however. Union forces had recently suffered a series of defeats. Seward felt the Proclamation would look like a "cry for help" from "an exhausted government." Lincoln agreed. He decided to wait for a meaningful Union victory to proceed with his plan.

The Battle of Antietam took place by Antietam Creek near Sharpsburg, Maryland.

WHAT ROLE DID THE BATTLE OF ANTIETAM PLAY?

On September 4, Confederate General Robert E. Lee attempted to invade the North. More than 39,000 Confederate soldiers crossed into Maryland. The Southern army was only 25 miles (40 kilometers) from Washington, D.C. On September 17, General McClellan's forces cornered the Confederates at Antietam Creek. The Battle of Antietam quickly became one of the bloodiest battles of the Civil War.

Both Union and Confederate forces suffered thousands of **casualties**. The battle was a draw. The next evening, Lee led his army back to Virginia. With Lee's retreat, the Battle of Antietam was a strategic Union success. Lincoln finally had his victory.

The president went back to work on the Proclamation. On September 22, he presented his advisors with a second draft. It was called the Preliminary Proclamation.

After winning the Battle of Antietam, President Lincoln wanted General McClellan to pursue the Confederate army and hopefully end the war. But McClellan refused. Lincoln removed him from command on November 5, 1862.

WHAT WERE THE CONDITIONS OF THE FINAL PROCLAMATION?

The Preliminary Proclamation included important points that were not in Lincoln's first draft. It declared that enslaved people in the Confederate states were free. It also added that U.S. armed forces would ". . . maintain the freedom of such persons." The U.S. government promised to protect the freedom and rights of formerly enslaved people in the South.

The Proclamation set a deadline for the Confederacy to make peace. The South had three months to end its rebellion. Otherwise, the Proclamation would take effect, freeing enslaved black people across the South. But the Confederates didn't surrender. So on January 1, 1863, Lincoln signed the final Emancipation Proclamation into law. The final Proclamation also allowed formerly enslaved people to join the U.S. military forces.

President Lincoln signed the final Emancipation Proclamation to become law on January 1, 1863.

FACT

President Lincoln considered the Emancipation Proclamation the most important part of his presidency. "If my name ever goes into history it will be for this act, and my whole soul is in it," he declared.

CHAPTER 3

What Did the Proclamation Achieve?

WHAT DID ENSLAVED BLACK PEOPLE DO AFTER HEARING ABOUT THE PROCLAMATION?

Many white enslavers tried to hide news of the Proclamation at first. But the news eventually spread across the South. Soon enslaved black people believed that freedom was possible. Before long, tens of thousands of formerly enslaved people fled and headed North to freedom.

HOW DID OTHER COUNTRIES REACT TO THE PROCLAMATION?

Early in the war, Lincoln feared that France and Great Britain would recognize the Confederacy as an official country. He didn't want them to aid the South in its fight against the Union. His fears didn't come true. Both France and Great Britain had previously ended slavery in their own countries.

Enslaved people in the South didn't learn about the Emancipation Proclamation right away. But Union troops gradually spread the news that they had been freed.

The Emancipation Proclamation gained approval in these countries and the rest of Europe. Lincoln's order helped prevent other countries from getting involved in the war. The South was unable to get any aid, which gave the Union a big advantage in the war.

HOW DID THE PROCLAMATION DAMAGE THE SOUTH'S FARMS?

During the war, most free white men in the South were busy fighting. Enslaved people did the hard work on farms that provided the food, clothing, and other goods needed by Southern soldiers and civilians. But after the Proclamation took effect, hundreds of thousands of former slaves fled. The South was stripped of its most important source of labor. As a result, Southern farmers struggled to keep people fed. It became impossible for the South to win the war with weak and starving soldiers.

After learning about the Emancipation Proclamation, thousands of formerly enslaved people traveled North.

What Were Contraband Camps?

By the war's end, nearly half a million former slaves had reached Union army lines. These men, women, and children were housed in **contraband** camps. The camps were located across the South in regions that the Union had captured. The former slaves gained the protection of the army, but life still wasn't easy. Black people suffered food and clothing shortages, overcrowding, and unclean conditions.

Women and children at a contraband camp in Baton Rouge, Louisiana

The 54th Massachusetts Regiment was one of the first all-black units in the Union Army. The soldiers played an important role in the Battle of Fort Wagner in July 1863.

HOW DID THE PROCLAMATION AID THE UNION?

Lincoln's order invited formerly enslaved people to join the Union Army. It encouraged them to serve at forts, on ships, and any other places soldiers were needed. For the first time, black people were allowed to serve in the U.S. military.

The boost in manpower was huge. By the end of the Civil War, about 200,000 black men served in the U.S. Army and Navy. Black soldiers served in the infantry and artillery. Many did noncombat jobs as carpenters, guards, cooks, and other roles. Women could not fight as soldiers. But many served as nurses, and some even worked as spies.

The efforts of free black men fighting in combat was very important. They showed that the purpose of the war was now to end slavery forever. Samuel Cable, a Missouri slave serving in the U.S. Army, declared, "I am a soldier now, to strike at the heart of this system that so long has kept us in chains."

Harriet Tubman is best known for helping enslaved people escape through the Underground Railroad. But during the Civil War she also worked as a spy for the Union.

FACT

The Union Army was not the only side to allow black soldiers. Weeks before the war ended, the Confederate Congress passed a law. It said that black men could serve in the Confederate army. However, in spite of their service, black soldiers would still be considered to be enslaved.

?

CHAPTER 4

What Did the Proclamation Fail to Do?

DID THE EMANCIPATION PROCLAMATION FREE ALL ENSLAVED PEOPLE?

It is often thought that the Proclamation freed every enslaved person in America. It did not. Lincoln's Proclamation declared that only enslaved people in Confederate states would be free. However, the U.S. government had no power in those states. The Proclamation couldn't be enforced there. Technically, the Proclamation didn't really free anyone in the Southern states. It only promised freedom if the Union won the war.

The Border States were not part of the Confederacy. The Proclamation didn't apply to them. It also didn't apply to some territories that had been captured by the Union. Lincoln purposely left out the Border States and captured territories. He hoped to maintain or gain the loyalty of white people in those places. He wanted their support to help the Union win the war.

The Emancipation Proclamation did not free enslaved people in the Border States. They were still considered to be property and were forced to work for white enslavers.

FACT

In the North, those opposed to slavery hoped the Proclamation would inspire enslaved black people in the South. They hoped it would spark a revolt against white enslavers. They believed a slave uprising would help the Union win the war. But a successful rebellion never happened.

After seeing the terrible treatment of enslaved black people in the South, many Union soldiers believed that freeing them was their duty.

WHY DID SOME NORTHERNERS OBJECT TO THE EMANCIPATION PROCLAMATION?

As expected, white Southerners were outraged by the Proclamation. But even some Northerners criticized it. Many opponents of slavery weren't satisfied. They wanted all enslaved people to be freed in the United States. But the document didn't do that.

The Proclamation also changed the focus of the Civil War. Many white Northerners supported the war to restore the Union. They didn't want to fight a war to free enslaved black people. Some soldiers in the U.S. Army felt the same way. Some even threatened to quit the army.

FACT
Most Union soldiers did feel that the Proclamation was necessary. As they marched through the South, they got to see the horrors of slavery firsthand. ". . . they quickly learned to hate it . . . they **resolved** that slavery must die." wrote historian Allan Nevins.

White people in the South were furious about the Emancipation Proclamation. They burned buildings and staged riots to protest what they felt was a violation of their rights.

WHY DID SOME PEOPLE FEAR THE PROCLAMATION?

The Proclamation raised fears for some people. Lincoln's order concerned enslaved people, who were considered property in the South. Some white people feared that the order could extend to their other property, such as land. But this fear never came true. Some people also feared that the Proclamation would cause the Border States to join the Confederacy. But they never did.

Many white people believed the Proclamation encouraged enslaved people to flee from the South. They thought that having so many formerly enslaved people move North would create conflicts with white people. Some feared that those conflicts would lead to a race war. Thousands of formerly enslaved people did escape northward. However, the predicted race war never happened.

After the Civil War, many formerly enslaved people moved North to support their families by working in factories.

CHAPTER 5

What Is the Proclamation's Legacy?

WHY WAS THE PROCLAMATION SO RISKY?

President Lincoln knew that the Emancipation Proclamation was a huge gamble. It could have been challenged in the courts and declared illegal. The Proclamation's success also depended on a Union victory. If the South won the war, the document would have been meaningless. Slavery would have survived. But Lincoln knew that the Proclamation was necessary. Without it, even if the South lost the war, white people would still have the right to enslave black people.

HOW DID THE PROCLAMATION LEAD TO NEW CIVIL RIGHTS LAWS?

The Emancipation Proclamation paved the way for a series of important laws. The Thirteenth Amendment to the U.S. Constitution permanently ended slavery in the United States. It was **ratified** in December 1865.

President Lincoln had worked tirelessly to pass the Thirteenth Amendment. But sadly, he didn't live to see it become law. John Wilkes Booth, a proslavery supporter, shot President Lincoln on April 14, 1865. Lincoln died the next day.

The Fourteenth Amendment was ratified in 1868. It granted citizenship to all people born in the United States, including former slaves. Then in 1870 the Fifteenth Amendment gave black men the right to vote. The Thirteenth, Fourteenth, and Fifteenth Amendments would change the country forever.

The Emancipation Proclamation was the first step toward granting black people the same rights as other U.S. citizens.

DID THE PROCLAMATION END DISCRIMINATION IN AMERICA?

Black people had gained their freedom. And slavery was no longer legal in America. In the first few years after the Civil War, black people enjoyed many political, social, and economic gains. However, by the mid 1870s black Americans still faced terrible **prejudice**. Conflicts with Southerners often turned violent.

In the South, state governments were often run by racist white politicians. They wanted to turn back the clock to pre-Civil War days. Southern states passed many Jim Crow laws. Many of these unfair laws forced black people to be **segregated** from white people.

Dr. Martin Luther King Jr. was a popular speaker and leader of the Civil Rights Movement in the 1950s–1960s. His work helped lead to the Civil Rights Act of 1964.

Other laws denied many civil rights to black people, such as the right to vote. The Jim Crow laws remained in place for many years. Finally, in the 1950s and 1960s, the Civil Rights Movement worked to put an end to the unfair laws. The laws were eventually overturned, guaranteeing equal rights for black Americans.

Although slavery ended in the 1860s, black people continued to face unfair treatment. The Emancipation Proclamation helped end slavery in America. But black people still faced many challenges. Did the Proclamation keep its promises? You'll have to look back at history and decide.

Important Civil Rights Events

January 1, 1863: Emancipation Proclamation issued

December 6, 1865: Thirteenth Amendment ratified

April 9, 1866: Civil Rights Act of 1866 is passed, declaring that all people born in the United States, regardless of race, are U.S. citizens

July 28, 1868: Fourteenth Amendment ratified

February 3, 1870: Fifteenth Amendment ratified

March 1, 1875: Civil Rights Act of 1875 becomes law, guaranteeing black Americans equal treatment in public transportation and public accommodations, and service on juries.

July 2, 1964: Civil Rights Act of 1964, bans employment discrimination on the basis of race, color, religion, sex, or national origin

More Questions About the Emancipation Proclamation

Why did Lincoln need the Emancipation Proclamation to be constitutional?

Lincoln wanted to end slavery, but he worried that a U.S. court could rule that the Proclamation was unconstitutional and strike it down. But as the nation's commander-in-chief, Lincoln argued that the act was "warranted by the Constitution, upon military necessity."

Did Lincoln view the Proclamation as a permanent plan to end slavery?

Lincoln realized the Proclamation wasn't a complete solution to end slavery. But it did guarantee that if the North won, the South would be forced to give up slavery.

Why did the Border States refuse Lincoln's buyout plan?

The Border States remained loyal to the Union, but they didn't want to give up their property. Enslaved black people were too valuable and important to the states' economies.

Abraham Lincoln

What was the reaction of the Border States to the Emancipation Proclamation?

The Proclamation didn't free enslaved black people in the Border States. But it still angered many white enslavers. They felt it was illegal for the government to control what they believed was their property. If the government could take away their enslaved people, it might take their other property as well.

GLOSSARY

abolitionist (ab-uh-LI-shuhn-ist)—a person who worked to end slavery before and during the Civil War

casualty (KAZH-oo-uhl-tee)—someone who is injured, captured, killed, or missing in a war

Confederacy (kuhn-FED-ruh-see)—the eleven Southern states that left the United States to form the Confederate States of America

contraband (KAHN-truh-band)—things that are not allowed; in the Civil War, runaway enslaved people who lived in Union-controlled camps were considered to be contraband

plantation (plan-TAY-shuhn)—a large farm where crops are grown; before 1865, plantations in the South used the labor of enslaved black people

prejudice (PREJ-uh-diss)—hatred or unfair treatment of people who are part of a certain group

ratify (RAT-uh-fy)—to formally agree to or officially approve

resolve (ri-ZOLVE)—to make a firm decision to do something

restore (ri-STOHR)—to bring something back to its original condition

secede (si-SEED)—to formally withdraw from a group or an organization, often to form another organization

segregate (SEG-ruh-gate)—to keep people of different races apart in schools or other public areas

unconstitutional (uhn-kahn-sti-TOO-shuhn-uhl)—when a law goes against something as set forth in the U.S. Constitution

Union (YOON-yuhn)—the Northern states that remained loyal to the United States and fought the Southern states in the Civil War

READ MORE

Byers, Ann. *The Emancipation Proclamation*. New York: Cavendish Square, 2018.

Cunningham, Kevin. *The Emancipation Proclamation*. Lake Elmo, MN: Focus Readers, 2020.

Morlock, Jeremy. *Abolitionists and Slave Owners*. New York: PowerKids Press, 2019.

INTERNET SITES

10 Facts: The Emancipation Proclamation
https://www.battlefields.org/learn/articles/10-facts-emancipation-proclamation

Abraham Lincoln
https://www.timeforkids.com/g34/abraham-lincoln/

Civil Rights: History of Slavery in the United States
https://www.ducksters.com/history/civil_rights/history_of_slavery_in_the_united_states.php

Emancipation Proclamation Facts
http://www.american-historama.org/1860-1865-civil-war-era/emancipation-proclamation.htm

INDEX